Scottish Castles

Photographs by
Colin Baxter

Text by
Bryn Havord

LOMOND BOOKS
EDINBURGH • SCOTLAND

Scottish Castles

The early years of Scotland's often turbulent history are partly shrouded in the mists of time, and historians are unsure about some of the events which took place in the country's formative years. From the beginning of time man's inability to live in peaceful co-existence with his neighbours has led to the need for him to build defences to protect himself and those in his care against a sometimes hostile world. The Scottish landscape is as rich as anywhere in Europe with mighty fortresses and fortified tower-houses providing tangible evidence of such endeavours.

In all probability it was during the Iron Age that the Celts established themselves in Scotland. They lived in tribes with an economy based on crops and animal husbandry. Their language, the precursor of the modern Gaelic and Welsh languages, allowed them to communicate with the early peoples of Brittany, Cornwall, Wales and Ireland. They lived in close-knit family groups and were conscious of the need to build themselves strong defensive positions for protection. They built hill forts in the Lowlands and from around the first century BC they built brochs, a new type of stronghold, in the coastal regions of the north and west on the mainland, in the Western Isles, and as far north as Shetland.

BLAIR CASTLE
Traditional home of the Dukes of Atholl, it was the last private castle besieged in Britain and was restored to its present appearance in 1869.

FYVIE CASTLE (opposite) A fine castellated mansion, which although founded in the thirteenth century, has many later additions.

BRAEMAR CASTLE
Built by the 2nd Earl of
Mar in 1628, it was put
to the torch by the
legendary clan leader
John Farquharson after
the Glorious Revolution
in 1688. It was rebuilt
around 1748 with a
round tower and star-
shaped curtain wall.

Their design was simple; a circular tower of dry masonry with cavity walls built to a height of perhaps 40 feet or more. From the outside they were almost impenetrable, with no dark corners for would-be invaders to hide in. Inside, they were usually built over a water source such as a well and contained ample living and sleeping space. An open fire provided warmth and heat for cooking. In Orkney there are over a hundred grass-covered remains of these intriguing buildings, and inside two that have been excavated there is evidence of stairways, galleries and narrow passages built into the massive defensive walls. The broch is unique to Scotland where there are the remains of at least five hundred. Dun Troddan and Dun Telve, at Glenelg Bay on the often stormy Sound of Sleat, face the Isle of Skye and are fine examples, as is Shetland's Mousa Broch. Edin's Hall Broch, to the west of Eyemouth in Berwickshire, is notable among the ten Iron Age brochs in the Lowlands.

When the Romans invaded Scotland they came overland under the command of Agricola. In AD83, after crossing the Solway Firth and sweeping through Dumfriesshire, Galloway and the southern part of Ayrshire, he and his legions crossed the eastern plain and built a fortress at

Inchtuthil in Perthshire as a secure base for further advances to the north. A year later he engaged the militarily undisciplined Caledonians in a battle which is referred to as *Mons Graupius,* the earliest recorded battle in Scottish history, where 10,000 Caledonians died with the loss of only 360 Roman soldiers. With the onset of winter Agricola was unable to continue his campaign. Instead, his fleet, which had earlier visited the islands and the west coast in the hope of finding easier access to the Highlands than the tortuous and dangerous overland route, was sent north to sail round the coast to prove that Britain was an island, exploring as far as the Orkney Islands.

Agricola was recalled to Rome by the emperor Domitian in AD85, and after his departure the Romans continued to maintain a presence in Scotland. Their earlier plans to occupy the Highlands were abandoned, and the decision was made to mark their northern boundary in Britain with the building of Hadrian's Wall, stretching from the Solway Firth to the River Tyne. Within twenty years of its inception Hadrian's successor Antoninus Pius decided to push the Roman frontier back into Scotland. He instructed that the Antonine Wall should be built across the narrowest part of the country between Bridgeness on the Forth and Old Kilpatrick on the Clyde.

The intention was to bring Lowland Scotland within the confines of the Roman Empire, but it was impossible to maintain the fiction of occupation for long, and within forty years of its completion the Antonine Wall was twice overrun by the Caledonian tribes. By AD297 all Highlanders were known as the Picts until a different occupying force, the Scots, crossed from Ireland in the fifth and sixth centuries. They settled in Argyll which became known as *Dalriada,* the kingdom of the Scots. Their language was Gaelic which gradually spread and came into common usage

MOUSA BROCH
Built around the first century BC, this broch on Shetland is a good example of these early strongholds which are unique to Scotland.

5

CASTLE STALKER
A well-preserved example of a sixteenth-century tower-house situated in a commanding position on the Lynn of Lorne.

BALVENIE CASTLE
During medieval times, this picturesque ruin was the moated stronghold of the powerful Comyn family.

among the Highlanders. Eventually, the name 'Scots' referred to all the people, and at this time, the country north of the Firth of Forth came to be known as *Alba*, the land of the Scots.

At the end of the first millennium it was not easy to survive as king and Duncan I was killed in battle by Macbeth in 1040. Macbeth became king until Duncan's son Malcolm Canmore took revenge, defeating and killing Macbeth in battle to become Malcolm III. During an unusually long reign from 1057 to 1093 he was constantly at odds with England's Norman rulers and at his fifth attempt to extend his kingdom into Northumbria he was killed at Alnwick.

With Malcolm's death in 1093 his sons David and Alexander went to England, where they grew up under the influence of the feudal world of the Norman court, which was in direct contrast to the patriarchal attitudes of the Scottish clan system. Alexander returned to Scotland to become king in 1107, but it was not until David succeeded him as David I in 1124 that the Anglo-Norman system of feudal land tenure and castles became a feature of life in the Lowlands. David spent his time at the court of Henry I and although his introduction of feudalism and the rule of law was not popular, especially with the clans, he became the most powerful twelfth-century Scottish king.

The early Norman castles were fairly basic constructions of earthwork and

timber in the motte and bailey style. The motte was a moated earth
mound on which a wooden tower, or keep was built, surrounded by a
stockade. The bailey, or lower court, was built onto the motte and was
also surrounded by a stockaded bank and ditch. This structure contained
the buildings of the lord's household.

In the towns of Elgin, Lanark and Peebles there are remains of this type
of administrative castle which was associated with the creation of
sheriffdoms and royal burghs. The design of medieval castles was not only
dictated by military and defensive considerations, but in a society which
was dominated by pomp and ceremony, the castle also had to symbolise its
owner's power and wealth. The castles were also the centres of local
government. They served as barracks for the soldiers, court room and
prison, and as a guest-house for visiting noblemen and dignitaries.

The experiences of the knights in the Middle East during the Crusades
influenced thinking about castle architecture. They were confronted with
massive stone castles and fortified towns which were more sophisticated
than anything they had encountered before, and against which their
assaults and siege machines proved to be ineffective, leading them to

INVERARAY CASTLE
The hereditary seat of the
chiefs of the Clan
Campbell, Dukes of
Argyll since 1400. The
present building is a fine
example of Gothic
revival architecture. It
was designed by Robert
Adam for the 3rd Duke
and completed in 1780.

*LOCHRANZA
CASTLE*
*An unusual structure
with two square towers,
it was built on the Isle of
Arran at the end of the
thirteenth century.*

BRODICK CASTLE
*(opposite) Viewed from
across Brodick Bay, this is
the ancestral mansion of
the Duke of Hamilton,
and an interesting
mixture of architectural
styles.*

drastically revise their ideas about the defensive capabilities of their castles
at home, and siege warfare in general. Castles became more vulnerable as
the technology of medieval warfare improved, with the siege strategists
devising ingenious contraptions to exploit the shortcomings in the basic
design of the structures. They designed machines capable of hurling rocks
and other missiles which damaged roofs and breached the tops of the
walls. The battering-ram was effective against the entrance gates, and
other breaches were made by sappers hewing their way through the
masonry, or burrowing under the bottom of the walls.

The castle architects and builders responded with new features in an
attempt to minimise or negate the effect of siege strategies and new stone
castles began to appear in Scotland at the beginning of the thirteenth
century. The massive stone walls were given refinements such as the
spreading, a sloping addition at the bottom of the wall, designed to keep
the sappers away from the wall proper, thereby exposing them to the fire-
power of the defending garrison if they attempted to breach the walls.
Moreover, the position of the castle became a more important
consideration to counteract the effectiveness of the siege machines, and

URQUHART CASTLE
*Positioned on a
promontory projecting
into the waters of Loch
Ness, this castle was
ideally suited to fulfil its
role as a base from which
its owners could
maintain their authority
in the Highlands.*

many were built on islands or peninsulas, making them almost inaccessible.

The Stewarts, who had been content to build wooden castles on their mainland estates, built a massive stone castle at Rothesay on the Isle of Bute. It is now one of the most important of the surviving medieval castles in Scotland. The original construction was a huge circular wall which enclosed the domestic apartments, and four projecting round towers were added later. The castle was stormed by the Normans when they successfully breached the walls, and a quarter of a century later the Norwegians captured the building through its two ill-protected entrances, meeting with little more resistance than boiling pitch poured from the top of the walls. They withdrew shortly after their victory, but King Haakon IV returned and recaptured the castle before the Norwegians finally ceded the feudal lordships of the Isles to Scotland.

The effectiveness of the design and construction methods of the new stone castles was put to the test during the War of Independence which was fought in the late thirteenth and early fourteenth centuries. The central figures in the War were the great patriotic leader William Wallace who helped to give impetus to the movement for Scottish independence, Robert I, known as Robert the Bruce, and Edward I – England's ruthless king who had already dispossessed the Welsh in an attempt to subjugate them. Edward was prevented from repeating the style of his Welsh castle-building campaign, where he built a ring of massive castles stretching from Aberystwyth to Flint, as he had depleted his treasury in his vain attempt to conquer Scotland. Nevertheless, in his campaigns he captured all the castles in central and southern Scotland which he then garrisoned with English troops who kept the local inhabitants under submission. He went on to win a battle at Falkirk in 1298 when, with a huge army of over 90,000 men, he defeated William Wallace, who lacked the support of the Scottish nobility.

In 1307, enraged by the reports of Bruce's success in a battle at Loudon Hill near Kilmarnock, Edward, who was nearly seventy years of age and suffering from a debilitating illness, set out to crush the rebellion. Although his eventual epitaph was the 'Hammer of the Scots', Edward died on 7 July 1307, at Burgh-upon-Sands, overlooking the Solway Firth and the prize that had finally eluded him.

The Comyns, who were one of the most powerful of all Scotland's baronial families, built a chain of formidable castles on their northern estates which included Balvenie in Glen Fiddich and Cairnbulg Castle close to Fraserburgh Bay on the east coast. Strategically more important was their castle at Inverlochy near Fort William at the south-west end of the Great Glen. It was built in 1275 by John, Lord of Badenoch, known as the Red Comyn. He also acquired Castle Urquhart which stands in a commanding position overlooking Loch Ness near Drumnadrochit, following the death of Alan Durward, Earl of Atholl. When Robert Bruce

URQUHART CASTLE
Seen from the air, the natural rock configur- ations provide the ideal defensive site for this castle. The Red Comyn, who inherited the castle on the death of the Earl of Atholl, was probably responsible for rebuilding the original timber castle in stone around 1275.

STIRLING CASTLE
Built on an extinct volcano outcrop making it almost impregnable, this castle played an important role in the country's military history and overlooks the site of the famous Battle of Bannockburn.

proposed a rebellion against Edward I, the Red Comyn, who considered himself rightful heir to the Scottish crown, refused. Bruce later stabbed him to death at the High Altar in Greyfriars church at Dumfries. On 10 February 1306, within six weeks of the murder, Bruce became king, and dedicated his life to freeing his country from English rule. To achieve his objective Bruce had to recapture the castles held by the English, and in particular Stirling Castle, known as the 'Key to Scotland'.

Stirling Castle, built on the summit of a long-extinct volcano, dominated the lowest bridging point across the river Forth, an important strategic link between southern and northern Scotland, and the scene of many great battles. It was held by the English in 1297 and recaptured by William Wallace, only to be taken again by Edward I in 1304.

The ensuing battle for possession took place in 1314; Bruce's opponent was no longer England's ruthless soldier king but his weak son Edward II. Bruce was heavily outnumbered, but by attacking from dry, high ground, he left the English to flounder in the mud of the flood-plains of the Forth valley. One of the biggest threats was the fire-power of the feared English archers, but by using cavalry, Bruce crowded the English in on themselves,

and severely restricted their ability to use their weapons. The English who attempted to escape were in danger of drowning in the river Forth, or in the Bannock burn after which the battle is named. Bruce dismantled much of the castle after his famous victory to ensure that his enemies would be unable to recapture it and exploit its important strategic position against him in the future.

Among the oldest surviving buildings is the Palace, built by James V, one of the earliest Renaissance buildings in Scotland. Other main features are the central turreted gatehouse with its curtain wall and flanking towers, and James IV's Great Hall. On the Esplanade there is a statue of Bruce, and close to the castle gates stands the Church of the Holy Rude where the infant James VI was crowned. The young Mary was crowned as Queen of Scots in the castle's Chapel Royal.

The Comyn family held power right across the Highlands by building castles at either end of the Drumochter Pass: Blair Atholl in the south and Ruthven Castle to the north. The latter was subsequently demolished by the Hanoverians and replaced with a barracks. Blair Castle was first built around Comyn's Tower in 1269, and by the time of Mary Queen of Scots'

*BLAIR CASTLE
Comyn's Tower, built in
1269, formed the basis
for the present structure
which has been
extensively remodelled
down the ages. The
Royalist castle was
captured by Cromwell
during the Civil War.*

*EDINBURGH
CASTLE
The imposing and
dramatic castle
dominates the city's
skyline and occupies a
key position which has
been of military
significance since the
Iron Age.*

visit in 1564, the castle had been extended southwards to include the great hall. Cromwell's troops captured the castle during the Civil War, and in 1703 Queen Anne rewarded the family's loyalty to the crown by creating the second marquess as Duke of Atholl. During the Jacobite rebellion in the eighteenth century, the castle was held by the Hanoverians when it became the last private castle besieged in Britain, and General Lord George Murray, who had forfeited his inheritance by supporting Bonnie Prince Charlie, laid siege to what had been his own house.

Blair Castle is the traditional home of the Dukes of Atholl. The present Duke, who lives in South Africa, remains head of the famous Atholl Highlanders, Britain's only private army. The castle itself stands in impressive scenery and was restyled as a Georgian mansion in the middle of the eighteenth century. In 1868 the architect Sir David Bryce carried out further work when he remodelled the castle to reinstate its earlier appearance.

Edinburgh Castle, like Stirling, is built on an extinct volcano. It dominates Princes Street and the picturesque streets of the city's Old Town. There is evidence that it has been inhabited since the Iron Age, but its royal connections began when

*EILEAN DONAN
CASTLE*
*Although completely
restored in the 1930s,
this spectacular building
is the archetypal Scottish
Highland castle standing
in a breathtaking and
incomparable landscape.*

Malcolm III made Edinburgh his principal residence. Malcolm first
married Ingibord, widow of the Norse Earl of the Orkneys, but after her
death he married the saintly Margaret, great-niece of Edward the
Confessor. Margaret died in the castle in 1093 after hearing that Malcolm
and her eldest son had been killed in battle at Alnwick, and the tiny St
Margaret's Chapel which is the earliest surviving part of the castle, was
dedicated to her memory.

Edward I occupied the castle in 1296, but it was recaptured by the
Scottish army in 1313 when the Earl of Moray, the nephew of Robert
Bruce, scaled the rock and the castle walls with only thirty men to take
the garrison. Bruce instructed Moray to dismantle the castle in
continuance of his policy of rendering ineffective any building which
the English might recapture and use against him. He ordered that only
St Margaret's Chapel should remain intact. As the Anglo-Scottish wars
wore on the castle changed hands many times and it was eventually
refortified by Edward III. The Scots reclaimed it in 1341, and it was
taken from Mary Queen of Scots in the middle of the sixteenth century.
Today only the ruin of David's Tower dates from the defensive structure

built before the fifteenth century.

During the Civil War in 1650 Oliver Cromwell's troops captured the castle after bombarding it for three months. It surrendered again in 1689 to the Dutch Protestant William III after holding out for Catholic James VII of Scotland, the last of the Stuart kings. In 1745 when Bonnie Prince Charlie marched south with his Highlanders to the battle of Prestonpans he occupied the city and blockaded the castle. He failed to take it, and with their defeat and the collapse of their cause at the bloody battle at Culloden in 1746, many of the soldiers found themselves imprisoned in Edinburgh Castle. Bonnie Prince Charlie's assault was the last time the castle featured in the battles for Scotland, although it was used as a prison for French soldiers captured in the Napoleonic Wars. Since then the castle has been visited by successive British monarchs, and houses the Crown Jewels of the Stuarts, known as the 'Regalia' or the 'Honours of Scotland'.

Not all the castles which have featured in Scottish warfare have been as grand as those at Stirling and Edinburgh. Some have been little more than fortified tower-houses such as the picturesque Kisimul Castle, built on a rock standing in the appropriately named Castlebay on the island of Barra. It was originally built in the thirteenth century for the pirate-chief of the MacNeils of Barra, and was once the largest stronghold in the Outer Hebrides. Little of the original

KISIMUL CASTLE
The island fortress founded in the eleventh century for the MacNeils of Barra.

TANTALLON CASTLE
This former Douglas family stronghold stands on a dramatic promontory overlooking the Bass Rock in East Lothian.

DUNVEGAN CASTLE
In a commanding position overlooking Loch Dunvegan on the Isle of Skye, the castle has been the ancestral seat of the MacLeods of MacLeod for over 700 years and is still their home.

building survives, but the existing main tower is thought to have been constructed in the twelfth century, while the largest part of the castle was built in around 1420. In 1938, the 45th clan chief, who also happened to be an American architect, started restoration work which was finally completed in 1960.

Perhaps the most picturesque Highland castle is Eilean Donan. It stands on a rocky island in a spectacular setting near Dornie, at the junction of Lochs Long, Duich and Alsh. Joined to the mainland by a causeway and stone bridge, it was originally built c.1230 as one of Alexander II's defences against the Danes, before passing to the Mackenzies of Kintail, who became Earls of Seaforth. In 1719 it was held by Spanish Jacobites when it was heavily bombarded by the English warship the *Worcester*. The castle remained a ruin until early 1932, when Colonel MacRae-Gilstrap of the Macrae family, who had held Eilean Donan as hereditary constables for the Mackenzies, restored the castle to its original condition. It now houses a war memorial and the museum of the Clan Macrae.

On the nearby Isle of Skye stands Dunvegan Castle which has been the seat of the MacLeods for over seven hundred years and is still their family

home. The castle overlooks Loch Dunvegan, which is situated between the Duirinish and Waternish peninsulas, and from the castle ramparts there are views to the Western Isles. The name Dunvegan is thought to be of Norse origin but the curtain wall of the castle was built in 1270 by Leod, son of the king of the Isle of Man, who also built the dungeon and the sea-gate which was the castle's only entrance until the middle of the eighteenth century. These are the only visible remnants of the early castle as the building work undertaken during the last three centuries masks the original medieval appearance. The castle houses many relics including the massive sword of the 7th Chief, William, killed at the Battle of Bloody Bay off Mull in 1480, and a lock of Bonnie Prince Charlie's hair.

To the south on the Isle of Mull is Duart Castle, the ancient seat of the Clan Maclean. The original castle was built in the thirteenth century at Duart Bay in a commanding position overlooking the Sound of Mull, the Firth of Lorne and Loch Linnhe. In 1745 the castle was forfeited by the clan chief and not recovered by the family until 1911. It was then that work began to restore it to its present condition.

Further up Loch Linnhe, towards Fort William at Portnacroish, Castle

DUART CASTLE
Built on thirteenth-century Norman foundations, the family home of the chiefs of the Clan Maclean is strategically positioned at Duart Point on the Isle of Mull.

KILCHURN CASTLE
A lofty tower-house built by a kinsman of the Campbell Earl of Argyll, with seventeenth-century additions erected by the Earl of Breadalbane.

ARDVRECK CASTLE

Stalker stands on an island in the shallow waters of the Lynn of Lorne, with stunning views across the loch to the hills of Morvern. The massive rectangular keep is of sixteenth-century construction, and was possibly started by Duncan II, Stewart of Appin, and finished by his son Alan who died in 1562. Its upperworks were remodelled around the middle of the seventeenth century and it was used by James IV as a hunting seat. As with most other castles of the period it changed hands more than once; it was held by the Campbells until the fall of the 9th Earl of Argyll in 1681, but after prolonged negotiations and litigation reverted to the Stewarts in 1686. The castle was garrisoned by Hanoverian troops during the Jacobite Rebellion, at which time the Stewarts had to forfeit their estates to the crown for having taken up the Jacobite cause.

At the north-eastern end of Loch Awe stands the ruined Campbell stronghold of Kilchurn Castle. Sir Colin Campbell, head of the Breadalbane family which occupied the castle until 1740, built the keep in 1440. The north and south sides of the castle were build by Ian, Earl of Breadalbane, in 1693. In 1746 the castle was garrisoned by Hanoverian troops and in 1879, the infamous gale which wrecked the Tay Bridge blew down one of the castle's towers.

In the wilds of Sutherland, just to the north of Inchnadamph in the barren wilderness of Assynt, is the gaunt and ruined Ardvreck Castle built in 1591 as the seat of MacLeod of Assynt. It stands on a grassy point with the mountains of Ben More Assynt

towering as its backdrop. In 1650 Neil MacLeod betrayed the Marquis of Montrose to the King's enemies and his neighbours subsequently stole ten thousand head of his cattle stock and drove him out of Assynt. The castle was in the hands of Mackenzie of Seaforth until 1760 when it was bought by Lady Strathnaver who gave it to her son William, Earl of Sutherland.

Cawdor Castle stands close to the River Nairn, a few miles north-east of Inverness, and near the site of the battle of Culloden fought in 1746. It is famous for its associations with Shakespeare's Macbeth who was promised the Thanedom of Cawdor by the witches. The castle is also assumed to be the setting for the murder of Duncan, but none of the buildings date from Macbeth's time in the middle of the eleventh century. The central five-storey tower, considered to be one of the finest of Scotland's medieval buildings, was built around 1370. In 1454, King James II of Scotland granted the Thane of Cawdor a licence to build a fortified castle on the provision that it would always be kept ready for the king and his successors. The original castle is surrounded by buildings which were added during the seventeenth and eighteenth centuries.

CAWDOR CASTLE
Despite alterations and additions this magnificent five-storey medieval building is one of the earlier Scottish tower-houses.

CRATHES CASTLE
There has been a castle
on this site since 1323.
The double square tower
dates from 1553, and the
rest of the building, rich
in gables and turrets, was
completed in 1600.

Standing on moorland near Cock Bridge in Grampian is Corgarff
Castle. The castle was besieged in 1571 and later involved in the Jacobite
risings of 1716 and 1745. The sixteenth-century, gabled tower-house is
enclosed within an unusual star-shaped, loophole wall which was added in
1748. Later it was garrisoned and used as a military depot in the
authorities' battle against smugglers until the early nineteenth century.

The area to the north of the River Dee around Crathes, which is a few
miles south-west of Aberdeen and known as the Lands of Leys, was
granted to Alexander Burnett by Robert Bruce in 1323. The Burnetts of
Leys started building Crathes Castle in 1553 with the square tower. The
rest of the building, which retains some of the best features of any
Scottish tower-house, was completed between 1596 and 1600. By this
time, the need for strategic positioning and military strength was less
important, leaving the family free to indulge their more aesthetic tastes
and concentrate on the domestic aspects. This is particularly evident in
the supposedly haunted Green Lady's Room, the Chamber of the Nine
Muses and in the spectacular Chamber of the Nine Nobles; all have
magnificent painted ceilings, and the Long Gallery with an oak-panelled

CORGARFF CASTLE

CRAIGIEVAR CASTLE

ceiling decorated with heraldic carvings is unique in Scotland. The castle is surrounded by over five hundred acres of grounds, with beautiful walled gardens, massive yew hedges and one of the best assortments of trees and shrubs in the country.

To the north-west of Crathes is Craigievar Castle, built in 1626 by William Forbes, the prosperous laird otherwise known as 'Willie the Merchant'. Very similar in appearance to Crathes, but without any later additions, the castle looks down towards Leochel Burn with views across the Don valley. Inside there are decorative plaster ceilings, depicting mythical and biblical characters, which date from 1625, and in the hall, with its tartan carpet and upholstery, there is a superb rendering of the Stuart Arms above the Italianate chimney-piece. As with Crathes, the castle remained in the hands of the family who originally built it until it was presented to the National Trust for Scotland in 1962.

Balmoral, the British Royal Family's favourite Scottish retreat, is sheltered by wooded countryside on a curve of the river in Royal Deeside. Robert II had a hunting lodge here towards the end of the fourteenth century. Sir Malcolm Drummond built a tower on the site, and the

BALMORAL CASTLE
This present royal retreat epitomises the Scottish Baronial style of castle which dates from the middle years of the nineteenth century. Originally a hunting lodge, the present structure was redesigned by Prince Albert.

GLAMIS CASTLE
The original castle was
given to John Lyon, Lord
of Glamis, in 1376 – a
gift from Robert I when
Lyon married his
daughter. The tower
dates from this time and
forms the core of the
present building, said to
be Scotland's most
haunted castle, with
Macbeth numbered
among its ghosts.

Gordon Earls of Huntly bought the estate in the fifteenth century. When Queen Victoria and her consort Prince Albert visited the castle in 1845, the Queen described it as a 'pretty little castle in the old Scotch style'. Prince Albert subsequently bought the castle and its 24,000 acre estate. In collaboration with Aberdeen architect William Smith, he proceeded to create the present neo-Gothic or Scottish Baronial mansion in white granite. A few years after its completion Queen Victoria added Ballochbuie Forest to the estate.

Glamis Castle is the historic Tayside home of the Earls of Strathmore and Kinghorne, with impressive grounds which border Dean Water. There has been a castle on the site since the early middle ages and King Malcolm II is said to have been murdered in the original castle in 1043. In 1537, Lady Glamis was put to death for witchcraft and conspiring to murder James V, at which time the castle was forfeited to the crown, even though her innocence was posthumously established. It was subsequently restored to her son and has been held by the Strathmore family ever since.

The castle owes its present appearance to the 3rd Earl of Strathmore, who carried out most of the building work in the seventeenth century,

adding numerous turrets and
battlements, some of which are
reminiscent of the style of a French
chateau. The castle has had many royal
connections: the son of James VII of
Scotland, who was also James II of
England, stayed here in 1715, and it
was the childhood home of Queen
Elizabeth the Queen Mother, who gave
birth to Princess Margaret here in
1930. Reputedly it is the most haunted
house in Scotland, with one ghost said
to be that of Macbeth, endlessly
expiating the murder of King Duncan;
another is Earl Beardie who plays dice
with the Devil for the sin of gambling
on the sabbath. An unidentified Grey
Lady is said to haunt the chapel; a
tongueless woman has been sighted
rushing across the grounds tearing at
her mouth, and a ghostly madman has
been seen walking along the 'Mad
Earl's Walk' on the castle roof.

Caerlaverock Castle, near Dumfries,
is considered one of the best surviving
examples of a medieval castle – not just in Scotland, but in Britain as a
whole. Built around 1280, it was besieged and captured by Edward I
during his Scottish campaign.

In 1300 the castle was entrusted to Sir Eustace Maxwell who, in 1313,
far from impressed with Edward's son, changed his allegiance to Robert
the Bruce. The Maxwells extended the castle in the fourteenth century,
and at the end of the fifteenth turned the gatehouse into a tower-house,
building upwards, rather than following the Norman practice of extending
outwards in the style of a courtyard manor-house. An east wing with a
Renaissance facade was added around 1630, but the castle was later
besieged and captured by the Covenanters – the Scottish Presbyterians
opposed to Charles I's attempts to introduce his new Prayer Book – who
demolished the facade.

When the Hanoverians succeeded to the British throne, forts became

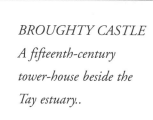

BROUGHTY CASTLE
A fifteenth-century
tower-house beside the
Tay estuary..

DUNNOTTAR
CASTLE
(opposite) This ruined
fortress was the last
Scottish castle to fall to
Cromwell's troops in the
Civil War.

*EILEAN DONAN
CASTLE
The Highland castle
reflected in the still
waters of Loch Duich.*

the new style military buildings, and by 1720 government redcoats under the command of General Wade were stationed at Fort William, Fort Augustus and Fort George along the Great Glen, the strategically important centres for keeping a tight grip on the Highlands. Wade built military roads between the forts and connected the network to the Lowlands, continuing the government's ruthless quest to subjugate the Highlanders. The most brutal and vindictive acts were perpetrated by George II's third son, the Duke of Cumberland. He was aptly named 'Butcher' Cumberland after the long and tragic struggle of the Highland clans came to an end with the defeat of Bonnie Prince Charlie at the Battle of Culloden in 1746.

*CASTLE STALKER
(opposite) The castle looks
across to the island of
Lismore, the seat of the
bishops of Argyll until
the Reformation.*

It is all too easy to overlook the bloodshed, betrayal and tragedy which have featured in the history of Scotland when looking at the dramatic silhouette of Eilean Donan castle in the light of a golden sunset, or when the early morning mist rising from Loch Linnhe swirls away to reveal Castle Stalker mirrored in the still waters, and a journey to discover these sometimes gaunt but enigmatic buildings could easily become a life-long obsession.

CASTLE FRASER, GRAMPIAN

LOCH AN EILEIN CASTLE, ROTHIEMURCHUS, CAIRNGORMS